W9-AOK-045

MY GUIDE TO US CITIZENSHIP

US LAWS OF CITIZENSHIP

Amie Jane Leavitt

Mitchell Lane
PUBLISHERS
P.O. Box 196
Hockessin, DE 19707
www.mitchelllane.com

MY GUIDE TO US CITIZENSHIP

Immigration in the US
US Immigration Services
US Laws of Citizenship
Your Guide to Becoming a US Citizen

PUBLISHER'S NOTE: The facts on which this book is based have been thoroughly researched. Documentation of such research can be found on page 45. While every possible effort has been made to ensure accuracy, the publisher will not assume liability for damages caused by inaccuracies in the data, and makes no warranty on the accuracy of the information contained herein.

The Internet sites referenced herein were active as of the publication date. Due to the fleeting nature of some web sites, we cannot guarantee that they will all be active when you are reading this book.

NOTE FROM THE AUTHOR: A special thanks to Wesley Biutanaseva, Fraser Smith, and Tania Rowland who agreed to be interviewed for this book. Your contributions were immensely appreciated and your experiences through the immigration and citizenship process helped provide a personal flavor to the text.

Printing 1 2 3 4 5 6 7 8 9

Library of Congress
Cataloging-in-Publication Data

Leavitt, Amie Jane.
US laws of citizenship / by Amie Jane Leavitt.
pages cm. — (My guide to US citizenship)
Includes bibliographical references and index.
ISBN 978-1-61228-448-4 (library bound)
1. Citizenship—United States—Juvenile literature. 2. Naturalization—United States—Juvenile literature. I. Title. II. Title: United States laws of citizenship.
KF4700.L43 2013
342.7308'3—dc23

2013023020

eBook ISBN: 9781612285085

PLB

CONTENTS

Words in **bold** appear in the Glossary.

US citizens include people from countries all over the world.

Who Is a US Citizen?

Just because a person is living in the United States or one of its territories does not mean that he or she is a citizen. Residency does not equal citizenship. There are three different statuses of people residing, or living, in the United States: **aliens**, **citizens**, and **non-citizen nationals**.[1]

According to the dictionary, the word "alien" has many different meanings. In this case, the word refers to a person who was born in one country, yet has moved to live in another country. Aliens can be either legal or illegal residents in a country.

If an alien moved to the United States legally, he or she went through the formal immigration process. This includes filling out stacks of paperwork, paying application fees, and having medical examinations, criminal background checks, and formal interviews. Often, it can take an applicant years to complete this process.

However, some aliens skip that lengthy process and come here illegally. They could do this by coming here as a legal temporary visitor and never leaving. Others might sneak over the border to enter the country.

People who are born in one of the country's fifty states or the District of Columbia are automatically United States citizens. People who are born in *certain* territories of the United States are automatically citizens of the United States, too. This is the case with the territories of Puerto Rico, Guam, the US Virgin Islands, and the Northern Mariana Islands.[2]

Citizens in the territories do not necessarily have the exact same rights as people born in the fifty states, though. They do not get to vote in federal elections. Their representatives in Congress do not have any voting power, either. While this may sound unfair, it's also important to note that people born in the territories don't have the same obligations as citizens born in the fifty states, either. For one, they are not required to pay federal income taxes.[3] This may sound like a good deal for the residents of these territories, but they are actually required to pay income tax to their territory's government instead.

So, do you have to be born in one of the fifty states or a certain territory to be a US citizen? No. You could also be born in a foreign country. How does that work? Well, let's say your parents were US citizens while they were overseas working, in the military, or just traveling. In this case, if you were born while your mother was in a foreign country, you would automatically be a US citizen.

Now, let's say that a person is born in another country and neither parent is a US citizen. Can this person be a US citizen? Well, not at first. But eventually, this person could if he or she went through the proper steps. First, that person

Visa Requirements for United States Nationals

- US states and territories
- Visa-free
- Visa issued upon arrival and/or visa-free upon arrival with payment of reciprocity* fee
- Visa required prior to arrival

*See Glossary for definition

The United States requires people from other countries to apply for and receive a visa before they are allowed to enter the country. United States citizens and nationals may have to apply for a visa before traveling to other countries as well. Each country has its own laws which regulate tourism and immigration.

would need to legally immigrate to the United States. Then, after a certain amount of time, the person could apply for citizenship. If this person is a good upstanding person and has followed all of the rules, then he or she could become a **naturalized** US citizen.

What if a US citizen adopts a child from another country? This child is a citizen as soon as he or she is adopted and enters the country. If the child moves to the United States with his new American family and is less than eighteen years old, then this child will be issued a Certificate of Citizenship.[4]

The US Citizenship and Immigration Services held a children's citizenship ceremony at their Fairfax, Virginia, office on November 14, 2011. Twenty-five children from nine countries celebrated their citizenship at the ceremony. Five-year-old Cynthia Newton (*left*) and her eleven-year-old brother James Newton became citizens during the ceremony. They were adopted by American parents and moved to the United States from their home country of Liberia.

Believe it or not, most Native Americans were not considered citizens of the United States until June 2, 1924. Before that time, only certain Native Americans were citizens, like those who had served in the military or who had married a US citizen. Even after they became citizens, though, some states still prevented them from voting. In 1975, Colorado and South Dakota became the last two states to finally allow all Native Americans to vote.[5]

So, who exactly is a non-citizen national?

In two of the United States' territories (American Samoa and Swain's Island), people are not given US citizenship automatically at birth. Instead, people born in these places are US non-citizen nationals.

A US non-citizen national does not have the same legal rights as a citizen. Instead, these people essentially have the same rights as a legal immigrant to the United States who is a permanent resident. A permanent resident has a **green card**, which is a document that gives a person the right to live and work in the United States. Permanent residents and US nationals also have access to Social Security benefits, can

Chiefs of Manu'a Samoa villages

attend public schools in the United States, and can join the armed forces. Just like immigrants who are permanent residents, US nationals can become US citizens. They just have to go through a specific process in order to do so.[6]

There is a lot of controversy regarding US citizenship among American Samoans. Some American Samoans think it's not fair that they are not automatically granted US citizenship at birth. After all, the US flag is flying over their land just as it does every other state and territory of the United States. They feel like they are being treated like second-class people. They don't believe the "non-citizen national" status gives them the rights and privileges they deserve. If they were US citizens, they would be able to vote in elections if they were living in one of the fifty states. They would be able to apply for certain federal jobs. They would also be able to travel freely from American Samoa to the Independent State of Samoa.[7]

Other people in American Samoa don't want that distinction bestowed on them. They feel that giving all American Samoans automatic US citizenship might threaten their traditional and cultural way of life.[8]

In 2012, several American Samoans sued the US government to gain citizenship rights for all American Samoans. The case created a lot of controversy among American Samoans, as not all of them wanted to become citizens. In 2013, a federal court dismissed the case and the plaintiffs decided to appeal the ruling. [9]

Citizens enjoy certain rights that non-citizens do not, like the right to vote. Because of this, hundreds of thousands of immigrants become naturalized citizens every year. In this 2008 naturalization ceremony in Los Angeles, California, 18,418 immigrants became citizens.

What Are the Rights of US Citizens?

There are certain rights that everyone enjoys in the United States regardless of whether they are an alien, non-citizen national, or a citizen. These are basic human rights that are protected by international treaties signed by the members of the United Nations.

The "Declaration on the Human Rights of Individuals Who Are Not Nationals of the Country in Which They Live" says that even if someone is not a citizen of a country, they should be treated fairly and justly. These people have the right to privacy and a fair trial. They have the right to choose a spouse and get married. They have the right to freedom of thought, opinion, and religion. They also have the right to bring their children and spouse into the country with them and to work in a safe and healthy place.[1]

While these rights are guaranteed by international law by the United Nations, not all countries honor these rights. There are some governments that treat their people very poorly and do not allow them these basic human rights. Many times, these people will try to immigrate to other places that follow international law. Refugees who immigrate to the United States often come here because their country is not safe and their governments do not protect their basic human rights.

All people in the United States are guaranteed all of the basic human rights described above. Yet, they also have even more rights, too. Many of these rights are described in the United States Constitution's **Bill of Rights**. The Bill of Rights is the first ten amendments to the Constitution.

The First Amendment grants people freedom of religion, press, and speech. It also allows people to get together in groups and discuss issues or **protest** government policies that they don't like. The right to own a gun is granted by the Second Amendment. The Third Amendment prohibits the government from forcing people to house and feed soldiers. The Fourth Amendment protects people from unlawful searches of their person or their houses. This means that the

The American Civil Liberties Union (ACLU) is a group that helps protect the rights of all people in the United States whether they are aliens, nationals, or citizens. When people feel like their rights have been violated, they can contact the ACLU and this group may help them pursue legal action. The ACLU lawyers can represent them in court and offer legal advice.[2]

government cannot come into someone's home to look around unless they have a signed order from a judge. The Fifth, Sixth, and Seventh Amendments grant people the right to a fair and speedy trial by a jury of their peers. They also explain that every person has a right to a defense lawyer in court. Because of the Eighth Amendment, a person convicted of a crime cannot be punished in a cruel or unusual way. The Ninth Amendment explains that the Constitution doesn't list *every* right that a person has in this country. The Tenth Amendment gives any power that is not specifically given to the United States government to either the individual people or the states.[3]

US citizens have other rights besides those specifically mentioned in the Bill of Rights. These rights include the right to vote, the right to run for elected office (providing they meet other criteria), and the right to apply for jobs in the federal government. Citizens also have the right to live and work in the United States, whereas tourists and certain immigrants may or may not have that right (depending upon their status). US citizens have the right to travel to other countries—as long as the United States and that country have good relations with each other.

United States Gun Law

Even though the Constitution says that people have the right to own guns, not everyone is allowed to do so. These are some of the people who are prohibited from owning a gun in the United States:

- People who have been convicted of certain felonies or misdemeanors
- People who are **fugitives** from justice
- People who are unlawfully using drugs
- People who have certain mental illnesses
- People who are non-citizens of the United States—unless these people are permanently immigrating to the country or have an exception such as a legal hunting license issued by the US government
- People who are in this country illegally
- People who have renounced, or given up, their US citizenship
- People who are under the age of eighteen (for long guns) and the age of twenty-one (for handguns)[4]

Home ownership is one of the dreams of many people living in the United States.

What Are the Duties of US Citizens?

Being a citizen of the United States is kind of like signing a contract with the United States government. The government promises certain things to the citizens (to uphold the citizens' rights) and the citizens in return promise to do certain things for the government. The things that citizens promise to do are called duties, or legal responsibilities. You may have heard the phrase "freedom isn't free." Citizens pay for their freedoms and rights by upholding their duties.

One duty that US citizens have is to pay their taxes. Many taxpayers cringe every time they think of their hard-earned money going off to some faraway government agency. Yet, taxes are necessary to keep the country running. Without money from taxes, the government could not pay its leaders, build and maintain roads, or offer emergency

It is the civic duty of US citizens to pay taxes. The US federal government spends and budgets tax dollars in many ways. In 2012, defense accounted for more federal spending than any other category. Defense spending held steady at 24 percent from 2007 to 2012. Health care spending comes in second.

services. The government also could not offer education through public schools and universities or provide safety services for its citizens. Paying taxes might feel like a burden for the citizen, but imagine how things would be if all of those services were not available. Because paying taxes is a duty, citizens could be fined or put in jail for refusal to pay taxes.

Another duty of an adult United States citizen is to serve on a jury. Juries play a very important role in the United States judicial process. After all, the Bill of Rights guarantees the right to have a trial by jury. That is why it is our job as citizens to serve on a jury when asked to.

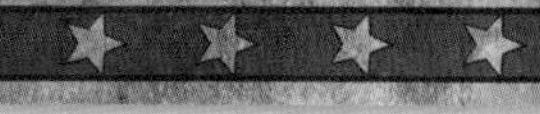

Naturalized Citizens' Perspectives: Fraser Smith, a naturalized US citizen who emigrated from Canada.

What do you feel like your duties are now that you're a US citizen?

I try to make a worthwhile contribution, not just because I'm an American, but rather as a member of the human race. I also vote (but I always did in Canada, too) and always pay my taxes. I also try to make a significant contribution through my career in the technical and education-related industry.[1]

At any given time, a US citizen could receive a letter in the mail stating that his or her name has been chosen to serve on a jury for an upcoming trial. This isn't a request. The person is required to do this by law unless he or she has a very good reason not to. It's up to each court to decide whether to excuse a citizen from jury duty. For example, if a woman is due to have a baby very soon, she may be excused from serving. If someone has a serious health problem, this person could be excused from serving. A person who is currently out of the country or soon to be out of the country may be able to serve at a later date instead. Someone who knows too much about the case would also be excused. Those are just a few of the reasons that a person might not be able to serve, and there may be others. However, having a job or not feeling like serving on the jury are not reasons to be excused. Your workplace *must* give you time off to serve on the jury and cannot penalize you for being gone. And as far as not feeling like doing it: that is no excuse. Serving on a jury is a civic duty.[2]

Another duty related to the courts is serving as a witness. If the courts **subpoena** you to give information about a criminal case in court, you are obligated to do so. You are

SUMMONS TO APPEAR FOR JURY SERVICE

By order of the circuit court of Cook County, Illinois, you are hereby summoned to appear for Jury service on the date and time at the court indicated below.

Failure to obey this summons may be punishable by a fine. **Please fill in the form on the reverse side of this summons and bring it along with you when you report.**

R. J. DALEY CENTER 50 W. WASHINGTON STREET ROOM 1700 CHICAGO IL 60602

JUROR NUMBER	SERVICE DATE	TIME
1234567	FRIDAY OCTOBER 14 2005	8:30 AM

BE PREPARED TO STAY UNTIL AT LEAST 4:30P.M.
BRING SOMETHING WITH YOU TO READ.
BRING CHANGE FOR VENDING MACHINES.
PLEASE READ "IMPORTANT INFORMATION FOR JURORS."
PLEASE DRESS APPROPRIATELY, SHORTS ARE NOT ACCEPTABLE.

JOHN DOE 583
1234 LINCOLN PARK AVENUE
CHICAGO, IL 60602-1234

Please Note: All of the courthouses to which Jurors are summoned are on the one day/one trial Jury system. If you are not selected to be a Juror for a trial, you will serve only one day and be discharged.

However, if you are in a courtroom for Jury selection at the end of the day or are selected to sit on a Jury, you must return to court every day until discharged by the trial judge.

Parking is not provided - Jurors must parkat their own expense.

Top: A sample summons to serve on a jury.

Bottom: An attorney speaks to a panel of jurors (*far left*).

not obligated to answer questions in the trial, however, if doing so will **incriminate** you or your spouse.

With a few exceptions, all male citizens and immigrants must register for Selective Service when they turn eighteen years old. "Selective Service" is a fancy name for the military draft. Just like paying taxes and serving on juries, registering for Selective Service is something that you *must* do. The only men who are excused from doing this are those who are continually hospitalized, in jail, or already serving in the military.[3] If a man refuses to register, he could be fined or imprisoned. Now, just because you signed up doesn't mean that you will serve in the military. It just means that if the

Registration Form

SELECTIVE SERVICE SYSTEM
Registration Form
READ PRIVACY ACT STATEMENT ON REVERSE
PLEASE PRINT CLEARLY

—DO NOT WRITE IN THE ABOVE SPACE—

1 DATE OF BIRTH — Name of Month / Day / Year
2 SEX — ☐ MALE ☐ FEMALE
3 SOCIAL SECURITY NUMBER
4 PRINT FULL NAME — Last / First / Middle
5 CURRENT MAILING ADDRESS — Number and Street / City / State or Foreign Country / Zip Code
6 PERMANENT RESIDENCE (If different than BLOCK 5) — Number and Street / City / State or Foreign Country / Zip Code
7 CURRENT TELEPHONE NUMBER — Area Code / Number
8 I AFFIRM THE FOREGOING STATEMENTS ARE TRUE — Today's Date / Signature of Registrant

Postal Date Stamp & Clerk Initials
☐ ID
☐ NO ID
☐ OTHER

SAMPLE

SSS FORM 1 (JAN 82)
(Previous Editions Will Not Be Used And Will Be Destroyed)
OMB Approval 3240-0002

At age eighteen, all American male citizens and immigrants (with a few limited exceptions) are required to sign up for Selective Service.

country goes to war and needs to raise an army quickly by drafting soldiers, they can call you up in a random lottery.

Citizens are also obligated by law to be loyal to the United States. If a person was to secretly work as a spy for another country, then this person (if found guilty in a trial) would be convicted of **espionage** or **treason**. These are very serious crimes of disloyalty against one's government. The reason these crimes are so serious is because they put every other person in the country (and maybe the world) in danger. If a person were to sell US secrets to another group or country, then those individuals could use that information to hurt our country, its leaders, or its residents. If a person is found guilty of espionage or treason in the United States, then he or she would be punished with prison time, loss of US citizenship, and even death.

Another duty that a US citizen has is to obey federal, state, and local laws. Laws are a necessary part of society. Without them, some people would do whatever they pleased without regard for the rights of others. Formal government would cease to exist and **anarchy** would be the result. If people choose to break the law in the United States, there are consequences. For one, some of their rights will be taken away. They could be imprisoned or fined which takes away their freedoms and property. If a person is convicted of a **felony**, then the person's Second Amendment right of owning a gun will be taken away forever, too. Convicted felons are not allowed to vote for certain lengths of time, which prohibits them from taking part in the democratic process. Along with obeying the law, US citizens are also required to support and defend the Constitution, and respect the rights, beliefs, and opinions of others.

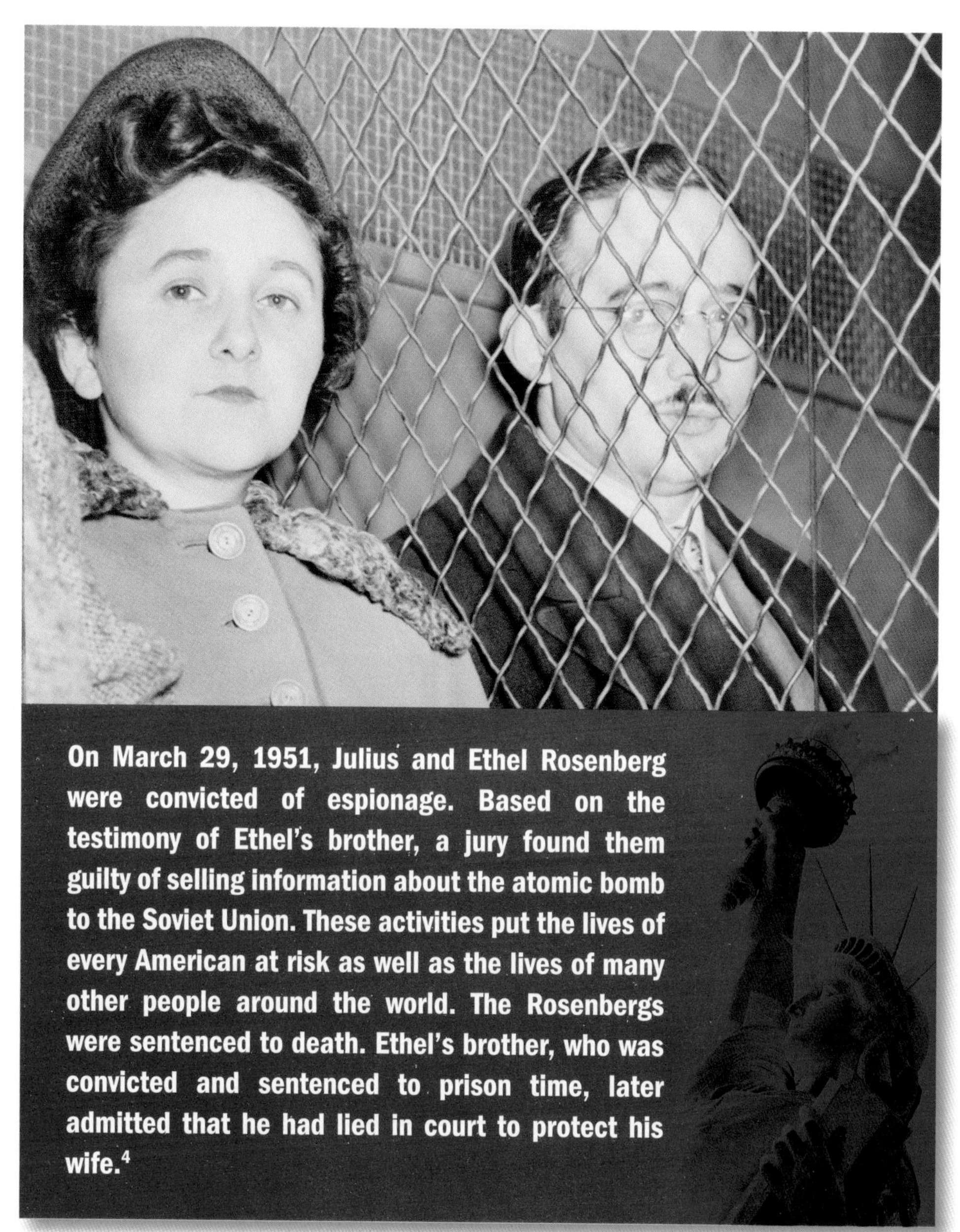

On March 29, 1951, Julius and Ethel Rosenberg were convicted of espionage. Based on the testimony of Ethel's brother, a jury found them guilty of selling information about the atomic bomb to the Soviet Union. These activities put the lives of every American at risk as well as the lives of many other people around the world. The Rosenbergs were sentenced to death. Ethel's brother, who was convicted and sentenced to prison time, later admitted that he had lied in court to protect his wife.[4]

It is important to stay up on current events so we know what is going on in our local communities, our states, our country, and our world. This knowledge helps us to be better participants in the democratic process.

What Are the Responsibilities of US Citizens?

In addition to legal duties, US citizens also have moral responsibilities. There are some things that we *have* to do because they are our duties. And there are other things that we *should* do because they are the right things to do. Those things we *should* do are called our responsibilities.

One of the responsibilities of a US citizen is to stay informed about important issues in the community and nation. A person can do this by reading the newspaper in print or on the Internet, watching the news on television, or attending political meetings. Why is this important? Think about it this way. If you don't know what's going on in your community or your nation, how can you possibly be able to make good decisions about important issues when it comes time to vote?[1]

Speaking of voting, that takes us to the next responsibility of a US citizen. We are not *required* to vote, so it's not our duty. However, we are *expected* to vote, so it would be considered our responsibility. Voting should also be considered a privilege. After all, there are many people in the world who don't get to choose their leaders and wish that they could do so. Voting is important for individuals, communities, and the nation. People who don't exercise their right to vote lose their voice in the government. And the only way that our

PENNSYLVANIA VOTER REGISTRATION APPLICATION

DO NOT WRITE IN SHADED AREAS

1 Are you a citizen of the United States of America? ☐ Yes ☐ No
Will you be 18 years of age on or before election day? ☐ Yes ☐ No
If you checked "No" in response to either of these questions, do not complete this form.

2 ☐ New Registration ☐ Change of Name ☐ Change of Address ☐ Change of Party ☐ I am a Federal or State employee and wish to retain my voting residence in the county where I last resided.
Place either Driver's License # or Social Security # here: DL # / OR SS# (last 4 digits)

3 Mr / Mrs / Miss | Last Name | First Name | Middle Name/Initial | Jr Sr II III IV

4a Address of residence, include street and city (Use map above if no street number or name) (If only P.O. box, see above) | Apt # | State PA | Zip Code

4b Telephone Number (Optional) ( )

4c Municipality where you live | County where you live

5 Mailing address (if different than address of residence) | City | State | Zip Code

6 Date of Birth / /

7 Race (Optional)

8a Name on previous registration

8b Address of previous registration | County of previous registration | Year of previous registration

9 In which party do you wish to register?
☐ Democratic ☐ Republican ☐ Libertarian ☐ Green ☐ No affiliation ☐ Other (Please specify):

10 Voter Identification Number ☐☐☐☐☐☐☐☐☐–☐☐

Place signature with full name (or mark) below. (Please see Penalty for Falsifying Declaration.)

X

11 I HEREBY DECLARE THAT:
(1)On the day of the next election I will have been a **United States citizen** for at least one month, I will be **at least 18 years of age**, and I will have **resided in Pennsylvania** and in my election district for at least 30 days;
(2)I am legally qualified to vote.
AND I HEREBY AFFIRM THAT the information I have provided in this registration declaration is true. I understand that this registration declaration will be accepted for all purposes as the equivalent of an affidavit; and if the registration contains a materially false statement, I will be subject to penalties for perjury.

Print Your Name Below | Date / /

12 Name of person who assisted in the completion of this application | Telephone No. | Address

DATE OF REGISTRATION | REGISTRAR | YEAR | PARTY AFFILIATION

NAME | CITY, BORO, OR TWP. | WARD | DISTRICT | COUNTY VOTER I.D.#

SAMPLE

In order to vote, you must be registered. This is a sample of a Pennsylvania voter registration application.

government can represent the views of the people is if every eligible citizen actually votes. Voting is how we choose the leaders who create our laws. Sometimes we even get to vote for laws directly, too. Voting is important at all levels of

Voting is an important responsibility of citizenship, and one that many people take seriously. Through voting, citizens are given the opportunity to express their opinions by choosing their government's leaders.

government: on the local, state, and federal levels. In order to vote, you must register. This is true for both people who have been citizens since birth and people who have become citizens through naturalization.[2]

Another thing that people should do as US citizens is to get involved in their local community.[3] They can do this by joining community organizations that are doing positive things for others. This might mean volunteering their time at schools or being a good neighbor and keeping their neighborhoods and workplaces safe and clean. People can

Volunteering is a great way to help in your community. For American citizens, it is also a responsibility. But many volunteers find that helping others is enjoyable and rewarding, too.

also do this by living with integrity, self-discipline, and empathy towards others.

What promises do new immigrants make when they become US citizens?

- give up loyalty to other countries
- defend the Constitution and laws of the United States
- obey the laws of the United States
- serve in the US military (if needed)
- serve (do important work for) the nation (if needed)
- be loyal to the United States[4]

People who have been born US citizens probably don't realize how important it is for them to know and understand information about the government of the United States. People who come here as immigrants definitely know about this, though.

In order to become a naturalized US citizen, a person has to take a test. This test has one hundred possible questions, including questions about the US government, US geography, and US history. The immigrant doesn't have to answer all one hundred questions. He or she only needs to answer six out of ten questions correctly. But since the immigrant doesn't know exactly what questions will be asked, he or she must study all one hundred questions and know them very well. About 97.5 percent of all immigrants pass this test every year.[5]

According to a study by Xavier University, native-born adult citizens wouldn't do as well on this test. Of more than one thousand native-born adult citizens who took the test in the study, only 65 percent passed. It's disappointing that people born in this country do not know more about their own country and government. Most could not even answer basic questions about our government.[6]

Here are some examples from the Xavier University study:

- **What is the supreme law of the land?** ***(Answer: the Constitution)***
  Only 29 percent of the people in the study answered this question correctly.
- **Who is the Governor of your state now?** ***(Answers vary by state)***
  Only 38 percent of the people knew the name of their state's governor.
- **What do we call the first ten amendments to the Constitution?** ***(Answer: the Bill of Rights)***
  Only 58 percent of the people knew the answer to this question.
- **What does the judicial branch do?** ***(One possible answer: decides if a law goes against the Constitution)***
  Only 25 percent of the people knew one function of the judicial branch, or court system, of the United States.
- **When was the Constitution written?** ***(Answer: 1787)***
  Only 9 percent of the people tested knew this answer.
- **What is the "rule of law"?** ***(Answer: Everyone must follow the law.)***
  Only 15 percent of the people asked knew the answer to this question.[7]

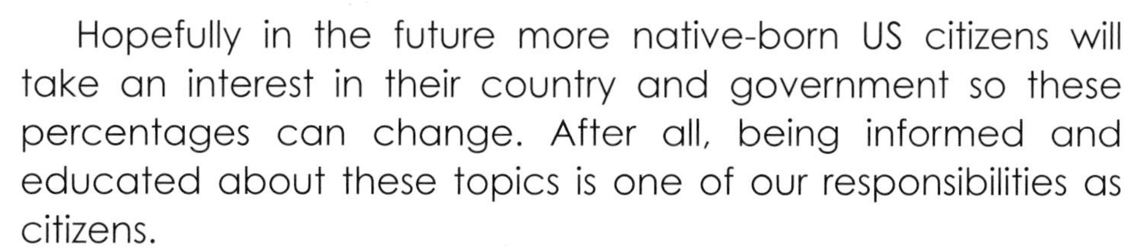

Hopefully in the future more native-born US citizens will take an interest in their country and government so these percentages can change. After all, being informed and educated about these topics is one of our responsibilities as citizens.

If you'd like to be more informed about US history, government, and geography, there are many things you can do. A lot of this information is already being taught in your school, so you can learn just by paying attention and studying. You can read books on the topics. You can search the Internet for websites on the topics. You can even study the one-hundred-question test that immigrants are required to take. This can be found online. Just look up "Civics (History and Government) Questions for the Naturalization Test" on your favorite search engine. The questions and answers are available, and you can find flash cards as well. Take the test yourself. Then quiz your family members and friends to see how much they know. Turn your study into a game to make it more fun!

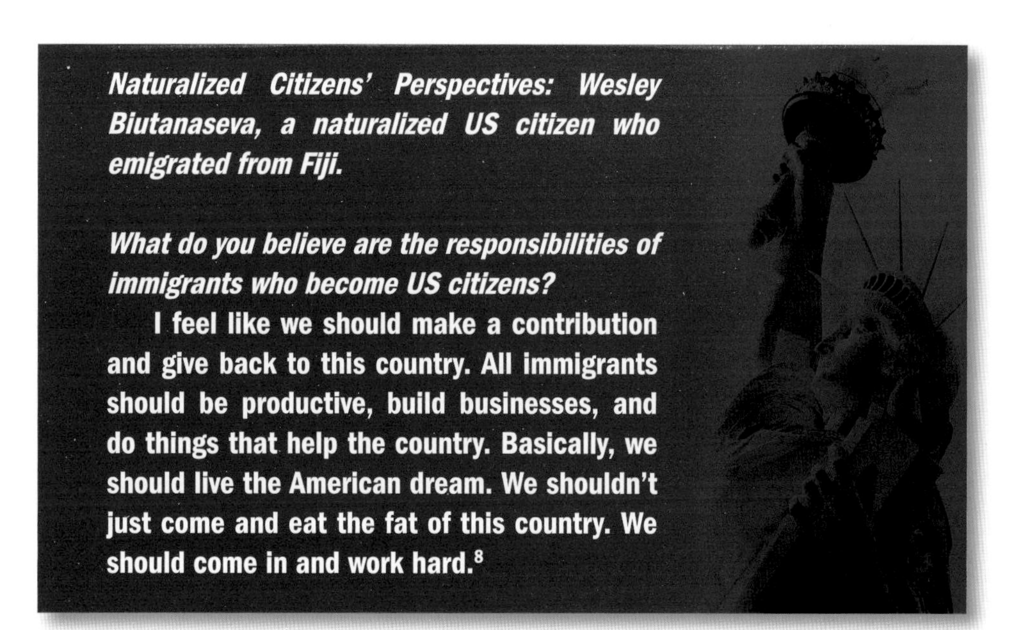

Naturalized Citizens' Perspectives: Wesley Biutanaseva, a naturalized US citizen who emigrated from Fiji.

What do you believe are the responsibilities of immigrants who become US citizens?

I feel like we should make a contribution and give back to this country. All immigrants should be productive, build businesses, and do things that help the country. Basically, we should live the American dream. We shouldn't just come and eat the fat of this country. We should come in and work hard.[8]

Some people volunteer to help immigrants study for their citizenship exams. In Littleton, Colorado, more than four hundred people volunteer at the Immigrant

Resources Center. Here, citizenship and vocabulary mentor Diane Hall (*left*) helps to prepare Korean immigrant Sanghee Lee for her citizenship exam.

Tania Rowland visited Disneyland with her husband and two children (Sabrina and AJ). When she was in her homeland of the Dominican Republic, Tania dreamed of coming to the United States and taking a trip to Disneyland.

From Immigrant to Citizen

People come to the United States as immigrants for many reasons. Many come for a better way of life. They know that there are many opportunities available to them in the United States that are not available to them in their homelands.

Tania Rowland is one of those immigrants. She immigrated to the United States from the Dominican Republic as a young college student and eventually became a citizen.

Here's a little of what Tania Rowland had to say about being an immigrant to the United States and a naturalized citizen.

Why did you come to the United States?

I wanted to come to the United States because I wanted to study and get a degree. I wanted to have better opportunities so that I could help my family in the Dominican Republic (DR).

What was it like for you to immigrate to the United States?
My experience was pretty good. I did everything legally and I achieved most of the things I had hoped to. I've been able to further my education, I learned the language, I have the career that I always wanted to have, I helped my family in the DR, and much more. I truly believe that the United States is the land of opportunities for everyone if they really try hard. I found my "American dream."

What was your experience becoming a US citizen?
For me, becoming a citizen was a must. I decided to do it for three main reasons: I wanted to help my parents get their green card faster. I wanted to be able to vote and have a voice in the United States. And I was so proud of being an immigrant to this country that I wanted to be a citizen, too.

What were the positive and negative experiences of immigrating?
There were so many positive experiences. I achieved a lot of my goals. I learned the language and graduated from college in the United States. I have a good life. I live in a good neighborhood and own a house. My kids go to good schools. I am able to help my family in the DR and, of course, last but not least, I got to go to Disneyland! The only negative part of immigrating is that I don't see my family and close friends in the DR as often as I would like.

The Dominican Republic is on the Caribbean island of Hispaniola. This country shares the island with Haiti. Christopher Columbus landed here on his first voyage to the New World.[1]

Tania and her family at Disneyland

What are the positive and negative aspects of being a citizen?

The positive is that I have a voice in the United States and I can vote like every proud American and have all of the rights of an American. I was also able to help my parents get their green cards. Honestly, I don't have anything negative to say. I love living in the United States.

How is your life different as a citizen?

I have all the rights that any American has. I am able to travel freely without any restrictions on time or places. I have a much better quality of life than I did in the DR. Even in a bad economy, the US money goes further and gets me much more than the money would have in the DR.

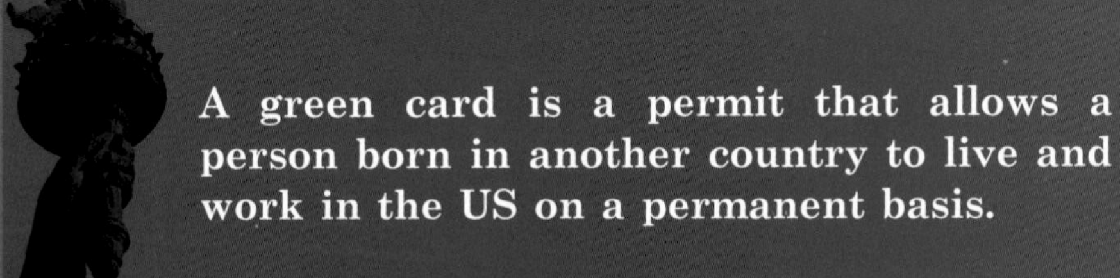

Do you think they should make it easier or harder to immigrate to the United States? Why?

Neither one, the immigration laws need to be changed so that we get more people who want to be part of the American society and fewer people who want to exploit this country or engage in criminal activities.

From your experience, why do people want to immigrate to the US?

They immigrate to have a better life and to become part of the American dream.

Why do people come to the United States illegally?
People come here illegally because the conditions in their countries are much worse.

Do you think this hurts the process for people who come here legally? Or does it not make a difference?
Yes, it totally hurts the process. It makes Americans leery of all immigrants. A lot of Americans think that all immigrants are illegal. . . . Also, a lot of the time, the United States is not letting the right people in. Our government spends millions trying to deport decent, honest, and hardworking people instead of worrying about deporting those immigrants that don't follow the rules of this country.[2]

Tania is one of many immigrants who have come to the United States and are making a significant contribution to the nation's culture, society, and economy. The United States is a country of immigrants that benefits greatly from the positive qualities that people from other countries bring here.

It doesn't matter if people are native-born US citizens, naturalized citizens, or citizens through adoption. Every citizen can have a positive impact on the country. They can do so by learning about the rights, duties, and responsibilities of US citizenship and **adhering** to all of them.

Will you be one of these citizens making a positive difference? Only you can decide that!

In February 2011, New America Media took a poll of immigrant women. Ninety percent of all female immigrants from Latin American and Arab nations wanted to become US citizens.[3]

Chapter 1: Who Is a US Citizen?

1. Superintendent of Documents, US Government Printing Office, *Ben's Guide to US Government for Kids*, "Citizenship," April 6, 2000, http://bensguide.gpo.gov/3-5/citizenship/
2. Free Application for Federal Student Aid, "Are You a US Citizen?" http://www.fafsa.ed.gov/fotw1112/help/fotw14a.htm
3. John Hood, *National Review*, "No Taxation Without Representation? Okay," March 12, 2009, http://www.nationalreview.com/node/178681
4. US Citizenship and Immigration Services, "After Your Child Enters the United States," August 9, 2011, http://www.uscis.gov/portal/site/uscis/menuitem.5af9bb95919f35e66f614176543f6d1a/?vgnextoid=c7070eaf3c4be210VgnVCM100000082ca60aRCRD&vgnextchannel=d0d049c62ed6e210VgnVCM100000082ca60aRCRD
5. American Civil Liberties Union, "Voting Rights in Indian Country," The Voting Rights Project, September 2009, p. 7.
6. AP News, *Bloomberg Businessweek*, "American Samoa Lawsuit Seeks US Citizenship," July 13, 2012, http://www.businessweek.com/ap/2012-07-13/american-samoa-lawsuit-seeks-us-citizenship
7. Constitutional Accountability Center, "*Tuaua v. United States*, Frequently Asked Questions," July 2012, http://theusconstitution.org/sites/default/files/briefs/Tuaua%20v%20%20United%20States%20FAQ%20FINAL.pdf
8. Associated Press, *Honolulu Star Advertiser*, "Gov Responds to American Samoa Citizenship Suit," July 26, 2012, http://www.staradvertiser.com/news/breaking/163858156.html?id=163858156
9. Ibid.

Chapter 2: What Are the Rights of US Citizens?

1. Rubrick Biegon, et al., University of Minnesota Human Rights Center, "The Rights of Non-Citizens," 2003, http://www1.umn.edu/humanrts/edumat/studyguides/noncitizens.html
2. American Civil Liberties Union, "Immigrants' Rights," http://www.aclu.org/immigrants-rights
3. "Bill of Rights," *Charters of Freedom*, http://www.archives.gov/exhibits/charters/bill_of_rights.html
4. US Department of Justice, Bureau of Alcohol, Tobacco, Firearms, and Explosives, *Federal Firearms Regulations Reference Guide*, September 2005, p. 226, http://www.atf.gov/files/publications/download/p/atf-p-5300-4.pdf

Chapter 3: What Are the Duties of US Citizens?

1. Fraser Smith, personal interview with author, December 2012.
2. United States Courts, "Jury Service," http://www.uscourts.gov/FederalCourts/JuryService.aspx
3. Selective Service System, "Selective Service—Who Must Register," http://www.sss.gov/PDFs/WhoMustRegisterChart.pdf
4. Rebecca Leung, CBSNews, "The Traitor," February 11, 2009, http://www.cbsnews.com/2100-500164_162-563126.html

Chapter 4: What Are the Responsibilities of US Citizens?

1. Bill of Rights Institute, *Americapedia*, "Responsibility," http://my.billofrightsinstitute.org/page.aspx?pid=1138
2. US Citizenship and Immigration Services, "Important Information For New Citizens," April 2012, http://www.uscis.gov/USCIS/Office%20of%20Citizenship/Citizenship%20Resource%20Center%20Site/Publications/PDFs/M-767.pdf
3. Ibid.
4. US Citizenship and Immigration Services, "Civics (History and Government) Questions for the Naturalization Test," March 2011, http://www.uscis.gov/USCIS/Office%20of%20Citizenship/Citizenship%20Resource%20Center%20Site/Publications/100q.pdf
5. Xavier University, "US Naturalization Civics Test: National Survey of Native-Born US Citizens," March 2012, http://www.xavier.edu/americandream/programs/documents/5CivicTestpowerpointfinalPDF.pdf
6. Ibid.
7. Ibid.
8. Wesley Biutanaseva, personal interview with author, December 2012.

Chapter 5: From Immigrant to Citizen

1. Robert Fuson, *The Log of Christopher Columbus* (Camden: International Marine, 1987), p.173.
2. Tania Rowland, personal interview with author, December 2012.
3. The Center for American Progress Immigration Team, "The Facts on Immigration Today," July 6, 2012, http://www.americanprogress.org/issues/immigration/report/2012/07/06/11888/the-facts-on-immigration-today/

Books

Hoffman, Mary Ann. *I Am a Good Citizen*. New York: Gareth Stevens Publishing, 2011.

Leavitt, Amie Jane. *The Bill of Rights*. Hockessin, DE: Mitchell Lane Publishers, 2011.

Loewen, Nancy. *We Live Here Too!: Kids Talk About Good Citizenship*. Minneapolis, MN: Picture Window Books, 2006.

Small, Mary. *Being a Good Citizen: A Book About Citizenship*. Minneapolis, MN: Picture Window Books, 2006.

On the Internet

Ben's Guide to US Government for Kids: "Citizenship"
http://bensguide.gpo.gov/3-5/citizenship/

Corporation for National & Community Service: "Serve in Your Community"
http://www.nationalservice.gov/serve-your-community

US Citizenship and Immigration Services
http://www.uscis.gov

US Department of Education: "Helping Your Child Become a Responsible Citizen"
http://www2.ed.gov/parents/academic/help/citizen/citizen.pdf

Welcome to USA: Celebrate Citizenship, Learn About America
http://www.welcometousa.gov

Works Consulted

American Civil Liberties Union. "Immigrants' Rights." http://www.aclu.org/immigrants-rights

American Civil Liberties Union. "Voting Rights in Indian Country." The Voting Rights Project, September 2009.

AP News. "American Samoa Lawsuit Seeks US Citizenship." *Bloomberg Businessweek*, July 13, 2012. http://www.businessweek.com/ap/2012-07-13/american-samoa-lawsuit-seeks-us-citizenship

Associated Press. "Gov Responds to American Samoa Citizenship Suit." *Honolulu Star Advertiser*, July 26, 2012. http://www.staradvertiser.com/news/breaking/163858156.html?id=163858156

Biegon, Rubrick, Michelle Collins, Scott Ferguson, et al. "The Rights of Non-Citizens." University of Minnesota Human Rights Center, 2003. http://www1.umn.edu/humanrts/edumat/studyguides/noncitizens.html

"Bill of Rights." *Charters of Freedom*. http://www.archives.gov/exhibits/charters/bill_of_rights.html

Bill of Rights Institute. "Responsibility." *Americapedia*. http://my.billofrightsinstitute.org/page.aspx?pid=1138

Biutanaseva, Wesley. Personal interview with author, December 2012.

Bureau of Indian Affairs. "Answers to Frequently Asked Questions."
http://www.dshs.wa.gov/pdf/esa/dcs/tribal/bia.pdf

Constitutional Accountability Center. "*Tuaua v. United States*, Frequently Asked Questions." July 2012. http://theusconstitution.org/sites/default/files/briefs/Tuaua%20v%20%20United%20States%20FAQ%20FINAL.pdf

Free Application for Federal Student Aid. "Are You a US Citizen?" http://www.fafsa.ed.gov/fotw1112/help/fotw14a.htm

Fuson, Robert. *The Log of Christopher Columbus*. Camden: International Marine, 1987.

Hanson, Mark. "Taxes as a Civic Obligation." University of Montana. http://www.umt.edu/ethics/imx/radioessays/comment_taxes.pdf

History. "Mar 6, 1951: The Rosenberg Trial Begins." *This Day in History*. http://www.history.com/this-day-in-history/the-rosenberg-trial-begins

Hood, John. "No Taxation Without Representation? Okay." *National Review*, March 12, 2009. http://www.nationalreview.com/node/178681

Leung, Rebecca. "The Traitor." CBSNews, February 11, 2009. http://www.cbsnews.com/2100-500164_162-563126.html

Office of the District Attorney, Orange County, California. "Witness Information." 2013. http://www.orangecountyda.com/home/index.asp?page=353

Rowland, Tania. Personal interview with author, December 2012.

Selective Service System. "Selective Service—Who Must Register." http://www.sss.gov/PDFs/WhoMustRegisterChart.pdf

Smith, Fraser. Personal interview with author, December 2012.

Superintendent of Documents, US Government Printing Office. "Citizenship." *Ben's Guide to US Government for Kids*, April 6, 2000. http://bensguide.gpo.gov/3-5/citizenship/

United States Courts. "Jury Service." http://www.uscourts.gov/FederalCourts/JuryService.aspx

US Citizenship and Immigration Services. "After Your Child Enters the United States." August 9, 2011. http://www.uscis.gov/portal/site/uscis/menuitem.5af9bb95919f35e66f614176543f6d1a/?vgnextoid=c7070eaf3c4be210VgnVCM100000082ca60aRCRD&vgnextchannel=d0d049c62ed6e210VgnVCM100000082ca60aRCRD

US Citizenship and Immigration Services. "Civics (History and Government) Questions for the Naturalization Test." March 2011. http://www.uscis.gov/USCIS/Office%20of%20Citizenship/Citizenship%20Resource%20Center%20Site/Publications/100q.pdf

US Citizenship and Immigration Services. "Important Information For New Citizens." April 2012. http://www.uscis.gov/USCIS/Office%20of%20Citizenship/Citizenship%20Resource%20Center%20Site/Publications/PDFs/M-767.pdf

US Citizenship and Immigration Services. "Welcome to the United States." September 2007. http://www.uscis.gov/files/nativedocuments/M-618.pdf

US Department of Justice, *Bureau of Alcohol, Tobacco, Firearms, and Explosives. Federal Firearms Regulations Reference Guide*. September 2005. http://www.atf.gov/files/publications/download/p/atf-p-5300-4.pdf

US Department of State. "Advice About Possible Loss of US Citizenship and Seeking Public Office in a Foreign State." January 1, 2013. http://travel.state.gov/law/citizenship/citizenship_779.html

US Department of State. "Birth of US Citizens Abroad." http://travel.state.gov/law/family_issues/birth/birth_593.html

Utah Education Network. "Citizen Responsibilities." http://www.uen.org/general_learner/civics/citizenship/responsibilities.shtml

Xavier University. "US Naturalization Civics Test: National Survey of Native-Born US Citizens." March 2012. http://www.xavier.edu/americandream/programs/documents/5CivicTestpowerpointfinalPDF.pdf

adhere (ad-HEER)—To believe in or follow something.

alien (EY-lee-uhn)—A person living in one country who was born in another country, but is not a citizen of the country they are living in.

anarchy (AN-ar-kee)—A state or society without government or law.

Bill of Rights—The first ten Amendments to the Constitution that guarantees the rights of individuals in the United States.

citizen (SIT-uh-zuhn)—A person who was born or naturalized as a member of a country and owes loyalty to that country.

espionage (ES-pee-uh-nahzh)—Spying.

felony (FEL-uh-nee)—A serious crime such as murder or burglary.

fugitive (FYOO-ji-tiv)—A person who is running away from the law because they have committed a crime or are suspected of committing a crime.

green card—A document or permit that allows a person to legally live and work in the United States on a permanent basis.

incriminate (in-KRIM-uh-neyt)—To present proof of a crime.

naturalize (NACH-er-uh-lahyz)—To give citizenship to an alien.

non-citizen national—A person who was born in a specific territory of the United States (such as American Samoa) but is not a citizen.

protest (PROH-test)—To speak in disapproval or objection.

reciprocity (res-uh-PROS-i-tee)—A fair exchange between two people or organizations.

subpoena (suh-PEE-nuh)—A legal document requiring a witness to appear in court or provide information in a case.

treason (TREE-zuhn)—A crime of disloyalty to one's government.

PHOTO CREDITS: Cover, pp. 1, 7, 25, 40—cc-by-sa; pp. 4, 9, 10, 11, 15, 16, 17, 18, 20, 22 (bottom), 24, 26, 30, 32—Photos.com; p. 8—Chip Somodevilla/Getty Images; pp. 12, 29—David McNew/Getty Images; p. 22 (top)—State of Illinois/US gov.; p. 23—U.S. Military/Selective Service; p. 28—State of Pennsylvania/US gov.; pp. 34–35—John Moore/Getty Images; pp. 37, 39—Tania Rowland. Every effort has been made to locate all copyright holders of material used in this book. If any errors or omissions have occurred, corrections will be made in future editions of the book.

About the AUTHOR

Amie Jane Leavitt is an accomplished author and photographer. She graduated from Brigham Young University as an education major and has since taught all subjects and grade levels in both private and public schools. She is an adventurer who loves to travel the globe in search of interesting story ideas and beautiful places to capture in photographs. She has written dozens of books for kids, has contributed to online and print media, and has worked as a consultant, writer, and editor for numerous educational publishing and assessment companies. Amie has a lot of close friends who are either first or second generation Americans. Because of that, she has had a great interest and appreciation for the immigration and naturalization process most of her life. It's for that reason, and because of her own heritage as a descendant of immigrants, that she particularly enjoyed researching and writing this book. For a listing of Amie's current projects and other published works, check out her website at www.amiejaneleavitt.com.